Just Write

Creativity and Craft in Writing

Book 1

Elsie S. Wilmerding • Alexandra S. Bigelow

Educators Publishing Service
Cambridge and Toronto

Acknowledgments

Many thanks to the second-grade students at the
Brimmer and May School for all their editing help with *Just Write,*
our first writing workbook.

Design by Persis Barron Levy

Educators Publishing Service
800.225.5750
www.epsbooks.com

ISBN 0-8388-2625-3
Printed in U.S.A.

6 7 8 9 10 VHG 09 08 07 06 05

Contents

Chapter 1
Getting Started

Brainstorming

Before writing a story, it is a good idea to **brainstorm** for ideas on what to write about. Our minds are filled with good ideas: brainstorming is a way of letting them out and writing them on paper in a simple way. Don't try to think about whether an idea is good or bad before you write it down. Just write.

Once you have some ideas on paper, you can then think about them, choose which ideas you like best, and get rid of the others. Then you can think of what you want to write about your favorite ideas.

•Listing

Making a list will help you remember the ideas you think of while you are brainstorming.

For example, here is a list of possible ideas I might write about:

> The circus clown
>
> A camping trip
>
> My new puppy
>
> A trip to Mars

In the back of this book are pages where you can write down some of your brainstorming ideas and story starters. If you ever get stuck trying to think of something to write about, you can look at that page to get started.

✎ Exercise

Now make a list of a few things you'd like to write about. Just go ahead and write! Later you can choose the ideas you like best.

Categorizing

Before writing, it is helpful to group similar ideas together. This is called **categorizing.** Grouping or categorizing similar ideas makes it easier to write a story that makes sense. For example, read this categorized list:

cow

hamster

parakeet

lion

wolf

✎ What do the words in this list have in common?

_____

_____

Here's another list:

going to the bike store

trying different bikes

choosing the purple mountain bike

picking out a helmet

✎ What do you think these actions have in common?

_____

- -

_____

So if you wanted to write about animals, it might help you to make a list like the first one. These might be all the animals you like. You could write a sentence about each one.

✎ Exercise 1

Look at the lists below. Find the item in each list that doesn't belong and cross it out.

1. science
   social studies
   running
   reading
   math

2. baseball
   soccer ball
   spider
   kickball
   football

3. summer
   shorts
   shirt
   pants
   socks

✎ Exercise 2

Think of something you do often, such as go to school, get ready for bed, or visit a friend. Make a list of some of the things you do to get ready. (For example, to go to school, you have to wake up first.) Write your list below.

_____   _____

- - - - - - - - - - - - - - - -   - - - - - - - - - - - - - - - -

_____   _____

_____   _____

- - - - - - - - - - - - - - - -   - - - - - - - - - - - - - - - -

_____   _____

_____   _____

- - - - - - - - - - - - - - - -   - - - - - - - - - - - - - - - -

_____   _____

Using a Web

A **web** is another way to brainstorm.

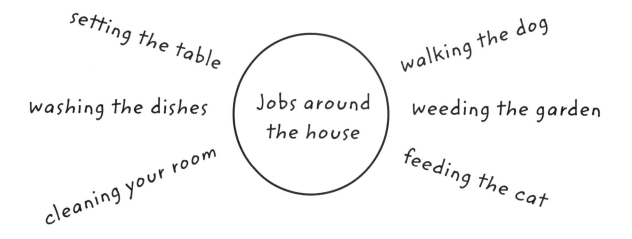

setting the table

washing the dishes

cleaning your room

Jobs around
the house

walking the dog

weeding the garden

feeding the cat

✎ Look at the web above and see if you can group the jobs into the following categories (groups):

Outdoor Jobs

_____

_____

_____

_____

Pet Jobs

_____

- -

_____

_____

- -

_____

Indoor Jobs

_____

- -

_____

_____

- -

_____

Remember, when you have grouped or categorized similar ideas, you will find that it is easier to write a story that makes sense.

Your story might end up like this:

> I have many jobs around the house. First of all, I walk the dog every day when I get home from school. Then I make sure the cat has her food. In the evening I set the table for dinner and help with the dishes. On weekends, my brother and I both weed the garden. I water the flowers in the front yard. He waters the ones in the back. Every Saturday I clean my room.

•Practice

✎ Look at the four different categories below. Read the words below and write each one under the category that you think fits best. Cross off each word below after you write it on a line.

Capture the Flag	hot dogs	wolf
chipmunk	boat	Frisbee
baseball	corn	ice cream
elephant	bike	airplane

Outdoor Games	**Food**	**Animals**	**Ways to Travel**

✎ Exercise 1

This time it is your job to think of examples for each of the four categories below.

Clothing	**Board Games**	**Sports**	**Musical Instruments**

Exercise 2

Now pick the category you like best from the ones in the previous exercise. Write three sentences using the examples you listed for that category.

My category is _____ .

Chapter 2
Writing a Story

It helps to follow a step-by-step process when you write a story. That way you won't get confused or forget things you want to write about. This chapter explains the different steps you can use to write a good story. The steps are

1. Topic

2. Sequence

3. Story Planning

4. Characters

5. Feelings

6. Setting

7. Problem

8. Conclusion

Topic

Every story has a **topic.** The topic is what the story is about. When you write a story, it is important to know your topic so that you have plenty to write about. It's also good to include plenty of details. Details give more information about your topic. For example, if your topic is your family's camping trip, a detail would be the waterfall you saw during a hike.

•Practice

Read this story to find the topic. Remember, the topic is what the story is about.

> When we decided to get a dog, we picked a terrier. They are small dogs with lots of personality. The color of their fur can be black, gray, tan, or red. Their ears are small and pointed. They always have a sweet expression on their face. They love people and hate being away from them. Terriers are very friendly dogs who love to play. They have lots of energy and sometimes behave like a puppy for many years.

Circle the words below that show the topic of this story.

1. a large dog   2. terriers   3. pet training

Exercise 1

Read this paragraph:

It was the first day of school. I felt nervous as I walked into the second-grade classroom. Ms. Ramos greeted us with a warm smile and a hug. That made me feel better. It was also great to see some friends in my class. Pretty soon Ms. Ramos asked us to sit in a circle on the floor for morning meeting. She began to tell us a little bit about second grade. I started to think that this was going to be a really fun year.

What is the topic of this paragraph?

When does it take place?

Where does it take place?

It's important to make sure that your sentences fit your topic. Look at these details below. Then write each detail under the correct topic.

eat cake

pack lunch

drive to the beach

open presents

get goodie bags

put on sunscreen

Cassie is eight years old today

go for a swim

The Birthday Party

A Day at the Beach

Read the story below:

When Sammy Squirrel woke up one morning, he realized it was very cold outside. When he peeked out of his nest, he saw leaves falling off the trees. He quickly kissed his mom and scooted down the tree. He knew he had an important job to do. He needed to gather nuts before the first snow. He dug down through the leaves and stuffed as many nuts as he could in his cheeks. He scrambled up his tree and put the nuts into his nest. By lunchtime, his mom said that he had gathered enough for one day and could take a break. He ran off to play with his friend, Sally Squirrel.

Now circle the sentence that best tells the topic of the story.

1. Sammy gathers nuts for winter.

2. Sammy Squirrel liked to play.

3. Squirrels live in trees.

Exercise 4

What is the topic of the following story?

Beth heard her friend, Peter, play a song on the trumpet. It sounded good! Beth wished that she could play an instrument, too. She knew there was a piano at home, so she asked her mom if she could take lessons. Beth wanted to be able to play real songs as soon as she could. Her mom said, "Yes, I know the perfect teacher. I will call her now." Beth was very happy. She wanted to start lessons right away.

The topic of this story is _____.

Read this story and think about the topic.

It was Matt's birthday. For the last two years, he had been asking for a pet. He was hoping for a puppy, a kitten, or even a hamster.

When he came downstairs to breakfast, his mom and dad were standing in the kitchen with big smiles on their faces.

"Happy Birthday!" they both sang out. There, sleeping on a large soft pillow, was the cutest little white kitten he had ever seen.

"The kitten is yours, Matt," said his mom. Matt couldn't believe it. He got his wish, a kitten of his very own.

Write a sentence below that tells about the topic of this story.

Read this story and think about the topic.

Mika's teacher, Ms. Jones, said that all library books had to be returned to school tomorrow. It was almost nine o'clock at night, but Mika still had not found her library book. It was way past her bedtime. As she lay in bed thinking, she remembered that the book was about a haunted house. It had many big and colorful pictures. Next door she could hear noises coming from her sister's room. Mika wondered why her little sister was still awake and making noise. Quietly she crept into Teni's room. Mika was very surprised, because there was Teni sitting in her little bed pretending to read and turning the pages of Mika's library book!

Now write a sentence that tells about the topic of this story.

Stick to the Topic

When you write, you should keep your ideas connected to the topic. You don't want to distract your reader with information that doesn't belong.

•Practice

Read this paragraph:

Yesterday I went skateboarding with my friend Anna. We went to the skateboard park that our city just built. Our city has a really great football team. The park is a safe place for us to ride our skateboards. We wear our helmets and pads in case we fall. Anna and I love skateboarding.

Did you notice the sentence that doesn't have to do with skateboarding? Cross out that sentence.

Exercise 1

Read the following paragraph. Cross out the two sentences that don't belong.

Yoko couldn't find her ball. She looked all around her apartment, and then finally asked her friend, Josiah, who lives downstairs, if she had left it at his place. Josiah's mother was getting ready to paint her kitchen yellow. Yoko and Josiah decided to walk to the park to look for the ball. When they got to the park, they went to the field where they had played kick ball the day before. A few weeks ago, they had seen a man there training a new puppy. They crawled under some of the bushes around the edge of the field looking for the ball. Then Josiah cried out, "Here it is!" Happily they pulled the ball out and starting playing with it again.

Using a Web to Organize Details

You already know that a web can help you brainstorm for ideas. A web can also help you organize your story. This web has details (more information) about the topic of the story. The writer picked a topic, wrote it on the lines in the middle of the web, and then brainstormed for details.

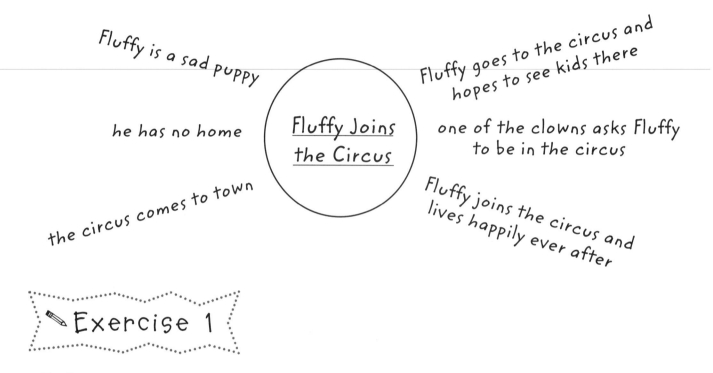

Fluffy is a sad puppy

he has no home

the circus comes to town

Fluffy Joins the Circus

Fluffy goes to the circus and hopes to see kids there

one of the clowns asks Fluffy to be in the circus

Fluffy joins the circus and lives happily ever after

✎ Exercise 1

Pick a topic, write it on the line in the middle of the web, and brainstorm for details about it. Write the details on the lines around the circle.

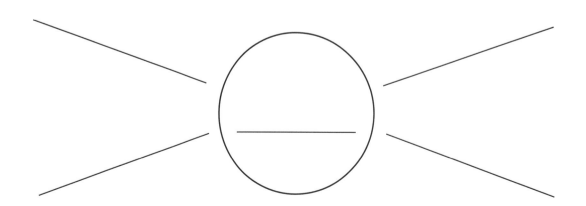

✎ Exercise 2

Now write three or four sentences about your topic. Use the details from your web in the exercise on page 18.

My topic is _____ .

_____

_____

_____

_____

_____

_____

_____

_____

_____

_____

_____

_____

_____

Sequence

When you write a story, it is important to tell what happens in the right order. For example, if you want to tell a story about your trip to the zoo, you probably wouldn't start by writing about the ride home from the zoo. Instead, you might begin by writing about the first animals you saw when you got there. The order in which you tell a story is called the **sequence.**

•Practice

The following events are not listed in the order in which they happened. Place them in the right order by numbering them from 1 to 5. The first sentence has been numbered for you.

___1___ Jake filled a bathtub with water and added dog shampoo.

_____ When Jake stopped scrubbing, Jasper shook and sprayed soapy water everywhere.

_____ Then he got Jasper, his dog, who was outside digging in the mud.

_____ He lifted Jasper into the tub and scrubbed him with a brush.

_____ When he was finished, Jake needed five towels to dry himself and Jasper.

The events in the following paragraphs are not in the right order. Number them so that we can tell the order in which they happened.

Ned's Puppy

_____ Marina and the puppy took a very long walk through the woods.

_____ Marina put the leash on the puppy.

_____ The puppy was so tired; Marina had to carry him home.

_____ Ned asked Marina to take his puppy for a walk.

Nini Is Missing

_____ Jen remembered she had taken Nini with her to the shoe store.

_____ The man at the shoe store found Nini.

_____ Jen's favorite doll, Nini, was missing.

_____ Jen's mom called the shoe store.

Making Cookies

_____ The cookies baked for fifteen minutes.

_____ Everybody ate a warm cookie with a glass of cold milk.

_____ They mixed the ingredients.

_____ Marie, Kenny, and Robert decided to make cookies with their mom.

Sequence Words

Sequence words help the reader figure out when something happened in a story. These are some of the most common ones:

before

after

first

second

next

then

last

finally

• Practice

Read this story and notice the sequence words that help you understand when things happened.

Mr. Prezzo likes to get up early in the morning. The first thing he does is turn off his singing alarm. Second, he jumps out of bed, goes to his bathroom, and splashes water all over his face. After that he shaves. He likes to sing lots of songs while he shaves.

Now finish the story about Mr. Prezzo. Use some of the sequence words to help you make the order clear to the reader.

Look at these pictures and see if you can tell the story in words. What happens first? What happens next? What happens last? For each picture, write a short sentence that tells what happens.

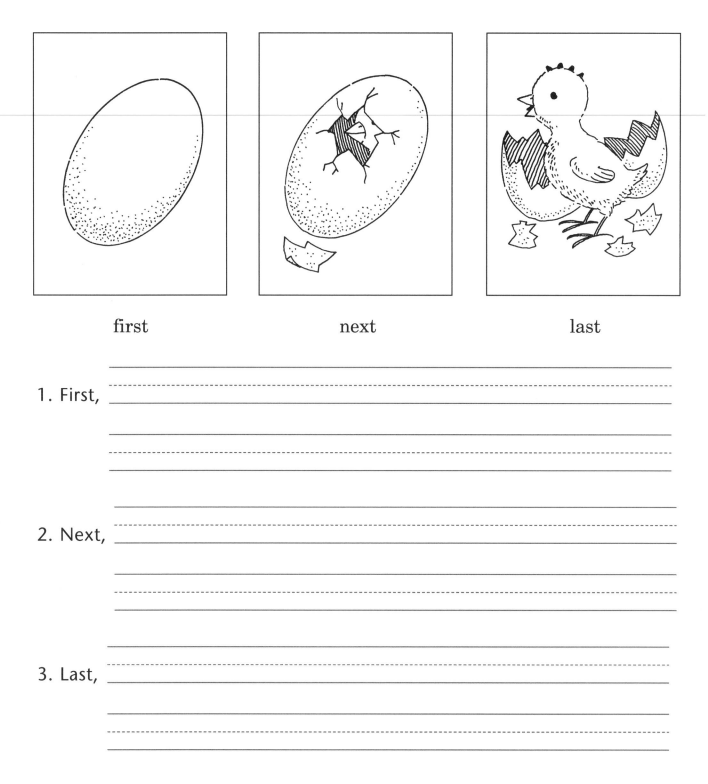

first   next   last

1. First, _____

_____

_____

2. Next, _____

_____

_____

3. Last, _____

_____

_____

These pictures are not in the right order. Write the words *first, next,* and *last* under the correct picture so that the pictures tell the story in the right sequence.

_____   _____   _____

Most people do certain things every morning. Here is a list of some. Write them on the lines below in the order that you would do them.

pack up my book bag

put on my clothes

wash my face

eat breakfast

brush my teeth

1. First, I _____ .

2. Second, I _____ .

3. Third, I _____ .

4. Fourth, I _____ .

5. Last of all, I _____ .

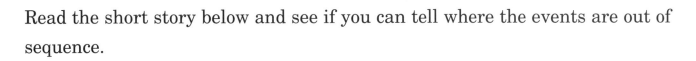

Read the short story below and see if you can tell where the events are out of sequence.

> Tami and Max decided to set up a lemonade stand at the Fourth of July parade. They asked Tami's Aunt Elena to help them. Pretty soon the crowd began to come. Before they set up the lemonade stand, they changed into shorts. They were happy that they made eight dollars and sixty cents. They brought a folding table, paper cups, ice, and two huge pitchers of lemonade to the sidewalk.

Now put a number next to each sentence to show what the correct sequence should be. Which sentence happens first? Which one happens last?

_____ Tami and Max decided to set up a lemonade stand at the Fourth of July parade.

_____ They asked Tami's Aunt Elena to help them.

_____ Pretty soon the crowd began to come.

_____ Before they set up the lemonade stand, they changed into shorts.

_____ They were happy that they made eight dollars and sixty cents.

_____ They brought a folding table, paper cups, ice, and two huge pitchers of lemonade to the sidewalk.

What should happen first?

_____

_____

What do you think should be the last sentence of this paragraph?

_____

_____

In this paragraph, the events are not told in the order in which they happened, but can you see how they still make sense? First read the paragraph. Then answer the questions.

David woke up in the hospital. His arm was in a cast and his head was pounding with pain. He tried to remember what happened. He had been riding his scooter behind his brother. There were icy patches on the road. He hit a bad spot and lost control. David remembered falling and crashing into the sidewalk.

What happened to David before he went to the hospital?

_____

_____

_____

What is the last thing David did?

_____

_____

_____

Exercise 7

Sequence words are especially helpful when you want to give someone directions or tell them how to do something. Write a few sentences to tell someone how to make a snack you like, such as a sandwich or popcorn or a chocolate milkshake. Think carefully about the steps involved. Use sequence words such as those in the box to help you move from one step to another. Make sure your instructions are clear so that anyone can make this snack.

| before | next | second | finally |
| after | first | last | then |

Story Planning

Before you begin to write a story, it is best to brainstorm for an idea, and then make a plan for your story. This will help you make sure you don't leave anything out.

How to Plan

Before you begin to write a story, it is best to make a plan. Here's how:

1. First, decide on the topic.

2. Then, write notes on the webs to help you brainstorm what happens in the story.

3. Finally, use your notes on the web to write the story.

Remember, a story web helps you organize and remember what you want in your story. You can make a web for each part of the story: *who, what, where, when,* and *why.* On the next page are some examples of webs used for the story about Matt's birthday present (page 15).

Topic: Matt's Present

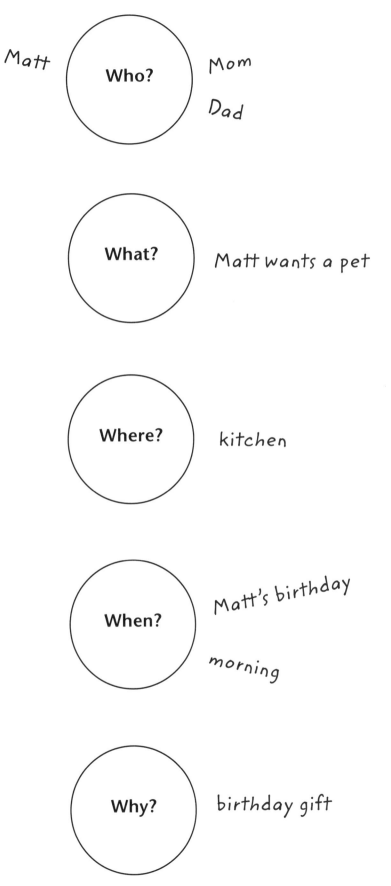

Matt   **Who?**   Mom

Dad

What?   Matt wants a pet

Where?   kitchen

When?   Matt's birthday

morning

Why?   birthday gift

A Sample Story Plan

Here is an example of how a story plan can be used.

Topic

How the Polar Bear Got His Fur

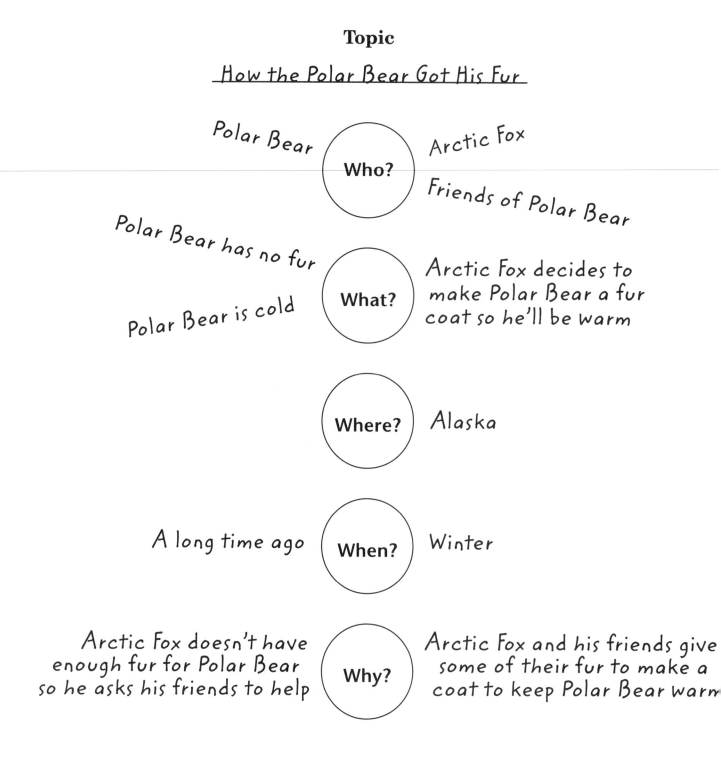

Polar Bear

Who?

Arctic Fox

Friends of Polar Bear

Polar Bear has no fur

What?

Arctic Fox decides to make Polar Bear a fur coat so he'll be warm

Polar Bear is cold

Where? Alaska

A long time ago **When?** Winter

Arctic Fox doesn't have enough fur for Polar Bear so he asks his friends to help

Why?

Arctic Fox and his friends give some of their fur to make a coat to keep Polar Bear warm

At the end of this story _Polar Bear is happy in his new coat._

Here is the finished story about How the Polar Bear Got His Fur. Look at how the words on the story map fit into the story.

It was an especially cold winter in Alaska. Polar Bear always had to cuddle very close to his friends to stay warm. Sadly, poor Polar Bear was always cold because he was born without any fur. His friend Arctic Fox tried hard to be patient, but every time Polar Bear cuddled up to him he could hardly breathe. He wanted to help his friend and make Polar Bear his very own fur coat, but he realized that he didn't have enough fur of his own to make one. What could he do? Just then he saw his other friends scampering about and noticed they all had plenty of fur and were toasty warm. Suddenly Arctic Fox realized that if he and all of Polar Bear's friends gave just a little of their fur, they could make him a fine coat. The friends agreed. The very next day all the animal friends gathered and knit the most beautiful fur coat. As soon as it was finished they rushed to give it to Polar Bear. He was so happy to be warm at last, but what made him the happiest of all was knowing he had such good friends.

A story idea has been started for you. Finish planning your story by adding more details to each web circle.

Topic: You are lost in one of these places (choose one):

a supermarket

a toy store

a museum

a spaghetti factory

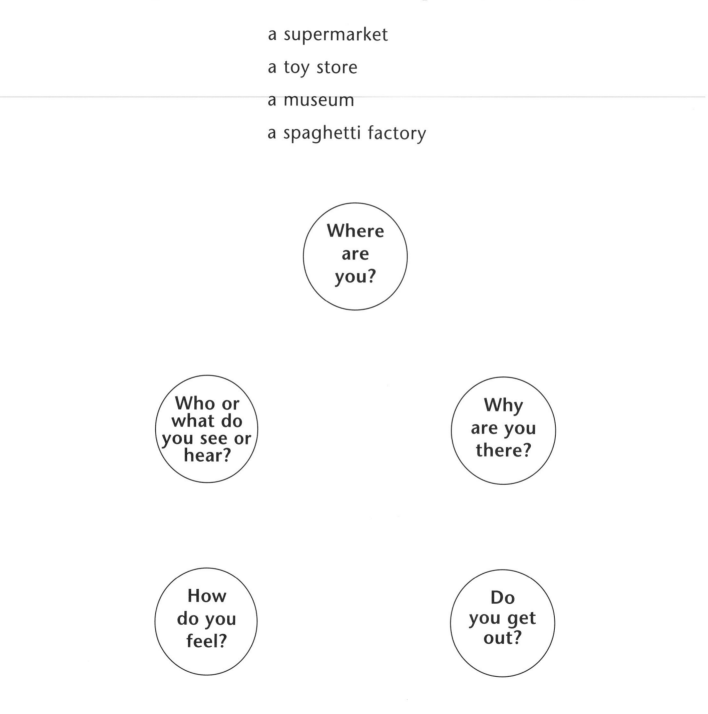

✎ Exercise 2

Now use your story plan to write your story about being lost.

Help, I am lost in a _____

_____

_____

_____

_____

_____

_____

_____

_____

_____

_____

_____

Story Plan

✎ Here is a blank story plan for you to use for your next story.

If you are not sure what to write about, you can use the list of story starters on page 140 to help you get started. If you know what you want to write about, make a story plan with an idea of your own.

Topic: _____

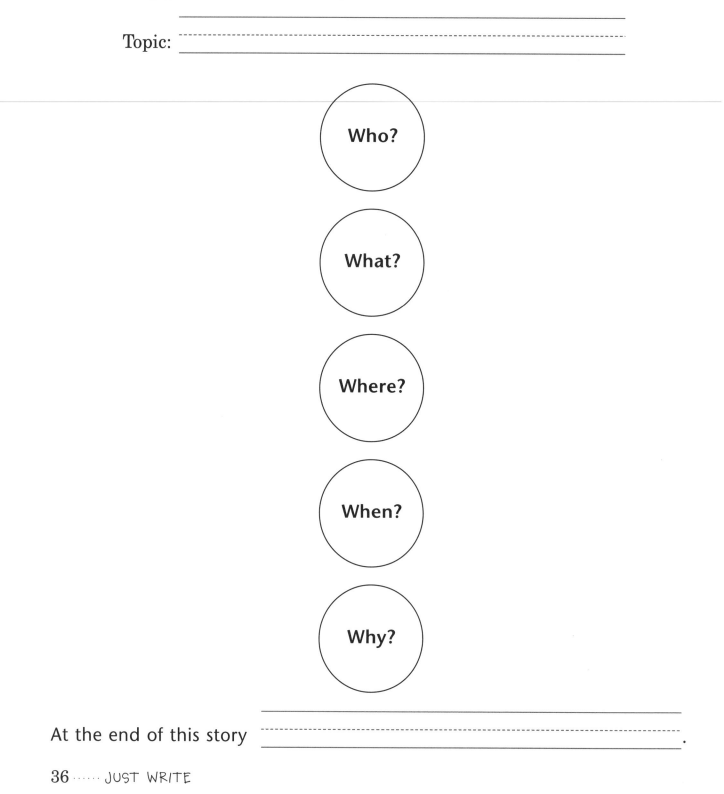

Who?

What?

Where?

When?

Why?

At the end of this story _____ .

✎ Exercise

Now write a story, using the plan you made on page 36.

Another Look

Think about your story by answering these questions. Later you'll have a chance to rewrite some of your stories and make them even better.

Exercise

Content Review: Topic and Sequence

1. What is the topic of your story?

_____

- -

_____

2. Write one detail you included to tell about your topic:

_____

- -

_____

3. What happened first?

_____

- -

_____

4. What happened last?

_____

- -

_____

5. What other sequence words did you use?

_____

- -

_____

6. What could you change in your story to make it even better?

_____

- -

_____

Characters

A story needs characters. Characters can be people, animals, or things with lifelike qualities. For example, in the story of Goldilocks and the three bears, Goldilocks and the bears are all characters. Without characters, a story is empty.

•Practice

Read the paragraph below and circle the names of the characters.

Seth woke up and tried to look out his window, but he could not see anything. It was too foggy and wet. He felt horrible, because today was the day that he and his friend Josh were going hiking. He picked up the telephone and called Josh. Seth told Josh that he thought it might be too wet for the hike. Josh moaned, "Oh, come on, let's go anyway. It will still be fun. My dad will come, and he will help us find our way."

"That's a good plan," Seth said.

An hour later, Josh and his dad pulled up to Seth's apartment. Everyone was excited, and off they went for the day.

Don't forget that animals can be characters also. Read the paragraph below.

Bert, the beaver, came home from a short trip. To his horror, he discovered that while he was away, a strong wind and fierce rain had destroyed his dam. He felt afraid and sad. Then he found his mother and father hiding with his baby sister under a fallen tree. His mother begged Bert to get help and find a way to move them to safety. Bert thought of his friend, Tuck, who lived up the river.

Bert set off right away to find Tuck. Together the two beavers worked hard. They built a new dam and carefully got Bert's family back to safety. Bert felt happy that he had such a good friend.

Who do you think is the main character?

_____

_____

Who do you think are the other characters?

_____

_____

_____

_____

Describing Characters

It's important to give your readers information about your characters. That will make it easy for the readers to picture the characters in their minds. A description tells about a character. A description usually talks about how a character looks and acts.

Read this description of Mrs. Curly:

> Mrs. Curly is my third-grade teacher. She wears thick glasses and has brown hair that is short and very curly. Mrs. Curly is always happy, and she has a wonderful bubbly laugh. All the kids in our class like her, because she tells funny stories, and she always says, "Nice job!" when we show her our work.

Did you make a picture in your mind of Mrs. Curly?

_____

- -

_____

Circle the words that tell what Mrs. Curly is like.

Now draw a picture of Mrs. Curly.

Using Details

Remember using the words *who, what, where, when,* and *why* to write story plans? You can also use those words to help you think of ways to make your sentences more detailed. Adding details can make your writing more interesting.

Read this basic sentence:

> The dog barked.

This sentence doesn't tell us very much. We know what happened and who did it, but that's all we know.

When did the dog bark?

> The dog barked last night.

How did the dog bark?

> The dog barked fiercely in the middle of the night.

Why did the dog bark?

> The dog barked fiercely in the middle of the night because he heard a noise.

Where was the dog?

> The dog on the porch barked fiercely last night because he heard a noise.

Remember, the dog is a character, so you can also describe what the dog looks or acts like:

> The large black dog barked fiercely and scratched on the door.

Notice how all of these sentences tell you more information than "The dog barked."

• Practice

When we write about someone or something, we want to make her, him, or it seem real. Details help bring characters to life.

Read this description of a boy named Zakir:

> Zakir is a boy in my class. I like him. We do a lot of things together.

✎ Does the description help you picture him? _____

Now read this description:

> Zakir is a boy in my class. He is shorter than the other boys are. His black hair is cut very short and it sticks straight up on his head. His ears are kind of big and stick out. He likes to wear blue jeans and sweatshirts. His sneakers are always untied. We love to play football. He can run fast!

✎ Why is it easier to picture Zakir when you read this description?

_____

_____

Draw a picture of Zakir using the details from the paragraph above.

Describing Yourself

✎ Practice

Imagine that you are writing a story about yourself. You want to make sure that your reader really knows what you are like. On the lines below, list lots of details to describe yourself.

Name: _____

Boy or girl: _____

Age and grade: _____

People in your family: _____

Size (tall, short, large, small): _____

Hair (color, length, curly, straight, etc.): _____

Eyes (color, size, shape, etc.): _____

Clothes you usually wear: _____

What do you like? (food, sports, games, school subjects, toys, and so on)

_____

_____

What do you dislike? _____

Describe your personality (shy, friendly, athletic, loud, energetic, quiet, and so on): _____

_____

_____

Using the details you wrote on the last page, write a description of yourself. Remember, besides describing what you look like, also include what you like and don't like. If you want, draw a picture of yourself on a separate piece of paper.

ME

_____

_____

_____

_____

_____

_____

_____

_____

_____

_____

_____

_____

_____

_____

_____

_____

_____

_____

Describing Animals

A good description of a character tells how they look and what they are like. It also includes how the character is feeling. This is true when you are describing any character, even an animal.

• Practice

Read the following character description:

> Floyd is an active one-year-old chocolate lab. He is a handsome dog with a soft and shiny coat. He loves people, especially Ned, his owner.
>
> Floyd woke up early one Saturday morning. Ned had not gone to work. As he waited patiently for Ned to wake up, Floyd was excited about the wonderful day he had in front of him. He knew they would go for a long run. He needed to stretch his strong, young legs. He loved fetching sticks. That was his favorite game.

Now circle the words that describe Floyd: the words that tell what he likes and how he looks, acts, and feels.

Think of an animal you'd like to write about. Make a web and write down four or more details about this animal. Write the topic in the center. Add more lines if you need to.

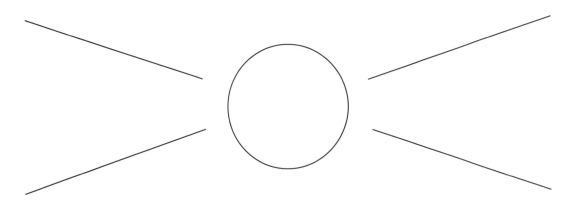

Now write a few sentences that include these details. Try to make it easy for your reader to picture the animal you're writing about.

_____
- -
_____
- -
_____
- -
_____
- -
_____
- -
_____
- -
_____

First, use this sheet to list some details about a monster that you create. Then give this list to someone so they can draw a picture of what your monster looks like. Be sure to have enough details so your partner has a clear picture in his or her mind of what your monster looks like.

Describing details about my monster:

Hair

Eyes

Nose

Ears

Head

Tail

Color

Body

Size

Hands

Feet

Mouth

Now draw what you think your partner's monster looks like.

I think _____'s monster looks like this:

Drawn by _____

Choose a character from the list below (or make up your own) and write it on the line in the web. Then write at least five details to describe your character.

Characters

boy/girl   firefighter

scientist   astronaut

detective   king/queen

magician   alien
                            ----

police officer

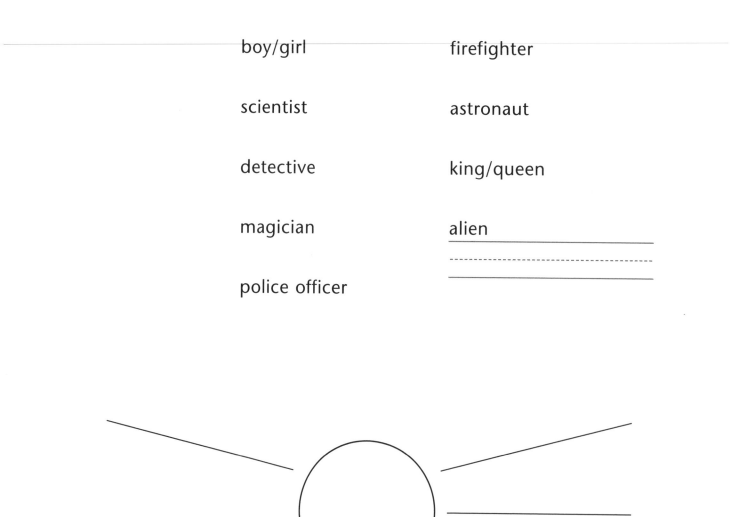

Now write a story about your character, using the details from the web.

Content Review: Character

1. What name did you give to the character you chose?

_____

_____

_____

2. Give two details you used to describe what your character looks like.

_____

_____

_____

_____

_____

3. Give two details you used to describe your character's personality.

_____

_____

_____

_____

_____

Feelings

When you imagine characters for your stories, you should think about how your characters feel. A character who shows feelings will seem more real.

•Practice

Read Justin's letter.

Dear Grandpa,

    I am so glad that you are coming to visit. Mom says that she will make a big picnic for us to take to the park. When we go to the park, you will get to see my new bike. You will be so surprised. The last time you came, I was still riding a three-wheeler. You won't believe what I am riding now. I'm excited to show you my new bike. Also, did you know that I could read? There are two books that I love. I can't wait to read them to you. I think you will be proud of me. How many more days until you will be here?

Love,
Justin

✎ How does Justin feel about his Grandpa?

_____

- -

_____

✎ Underline the words that show some of Justin's other feelings.

Read this story and see if you can tell how feelings can change.

Jake was nervous about going to the hospital. He was getting a cast on his leg, because he hurt it badly in an accident. As his mom drove to the entrance of the hospital, Jake felt a little sick and began to cry. Even though his mom said that everything would be okay, Jake didn't like hospitals. He felt scared and unhappy.

The next day, everyone wanted to write something on Jake's big cast. His mom and brother wrote their names, and when the doctor drew a funny picture, Jake smiled. He was excited to show his cast to his friends.

How does Jake feel? Circle the words that show Jake's feelings.

How do his feelings change?

_____

_____

_____

_____

_____

_____

Exercise 2

Read this short story and look for the words that tell about feelings.

My new school is great! We have two very long recesses. Also, there are many different team sports. We can choose which one we want to play; I like soccer.

This year, I love art. Today we made really funny masks, and the art teacher displayed them, so the whole school will see them. I have made lots of new friends. Moving wasn't so bad.

How does this student feel about the new school?

What are some of the details that show that he or she likes school?

1.

2.

3.

Read the sentences below. Try to imagine the feelings that the characters have in each of the sentences, and then describe the feelings.

1. Dad hopped out of his new car and whistled a tune as he walked into the house.

_____

_____

2. Maria sat on her front steps with her head in her hands. She had looked everywhere for her puppy.

_____

_____

3. My little brother screamed and hung onto our mother's coat on the first day of school.

_____

_____

4. Jack jumped up and down when he made the winning goal.

_____

_____

5. Leo got the same kind of bike that Teddy had been wishing for all year.

_____

_____

6. Keesha and Ali told Abby that she couldn't join the club.

_____

_____

Exercise 4

Read this story and fill in the blanks with words that show Rebekah's feelings. You may use the words at the top of the page or choose your own. Do not use a word more than once.

annoyed	miserable	shocked
impatient	terrified	excited
irritated	angry	astonished
scared	dismal	relieved
lonely	hurt	comforted
unhappy	surprised	

Rebekah was feeling _____ and _____ because there wasn't anybody at home for her to play with, so she went to climb her neighbor's apple tree. On her way up, she was _____ to see a robin's nest. She was so _____ to tell her dad about the pretty blue eggs inside that she didn't notice the branch bending below her. She slipped and fell to the ground. She lay there feeling _____ and _____ that nobody was there to help her. Then Rebekah saw her neighbor running toward her. Rebekah felt _____.

Choose two of the feelings below. Circle the ones you choose and then draw two faces that express those feelings.

happy

sad

surprised

angry

Now think of two other feelings, and write them on the extra lines below. Draw faces that show those feelings.

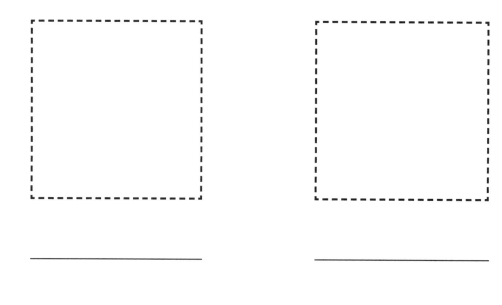

Exercise 6

Draw a picture of a person expressing a certain feeling.

Write on the line below what the feeling is:

Now write two sentences that tell more about this person and his or her feeling.

Make up a short story to describe why this boy has this expression on his face. Who is he? Where is he? What happened? Have him change how he feels somewhere in the story.

Here are some words that describe feelings. Circle the ones that describe the boy in your story.

happy	terrified
scared	sorry
relieved	confident
frustrated	overjoyed
miserable	lonely
comforted	angry
surprised	shocked
silly	determined

Setting

What is the **setting?**

The setting tells where and when the story takes place.

When?

Day or night?

Season?

Past, present, or future?

Where?

A crowded bus	Chicago	The zoo
A vacation spot	A grocery store	Out in the woods
A hospital	Outer space	Mexico

• Practice

Think about the setting in the following sentences. Look for words that will give clues about the time of day and the season.

> The little white fox darted across the open field in the moonlight. She left a tiny trail of footprints in the fresh snow. Not a single sound was heard as she scurried into the woods.

✎ What words tell us about the time of day?

_____

- -

_____

✎ What words tell us about the season?

_____

- -

_____

✎ What words tell us whether the place is in the country or the city?

_____

- -

_____

✎ Exercise 1

As you read this story, notice the details that let you know where and when it takes place.

> When I looked out the window, I could see Grandpa as he walked to the barn to feed the horses. The sun was just coming up over the mountains, but it was already hot. I was so excited that I was finally here. I had been looking forward to visiting my grandparents. I left on the first bus after school let out. I pulled on my jeans and cowboy boots. I couldn't wait to get outside to help saddle up the horses.

Where do you think the story takes place? _____

What time of year is it? _____

What time of day is it? _____

Read this story and think about the setting.

As I stepped out of the bus, I looked straight up. I couldn't believe how big the buildings were. It was amazing. The streets were filled with cars and trucks that were rushing around and honking their horns. The sidewalks were filled with people who were all bundled up and seemed to be rushing to get out of the cold. Suddenly, a snowplow whipped by, splashing me with wet snow from head to toe. I began to wonder if I had picked the best day for a visit.

Underline the words that tell when and where the story takes place.

Where do you think the story takes place? _____

What time of year is it? _____

Exercise 3

Here are two different settings. Read the words below and write them on the line in the correct category. Cross off each word below after you write it on the line.

streetlights   tall buildings   pine trees

dirt road   field   mountains

quiet pond   crowded sidewalks   subways

taxis   wildflowers   neon signs

A night in the city   **A day in the country**

_____   _____

_____   _____

_____   _____

_____   _____

_____   _____

_____   _____

_____   _____

✎ Exercise 4, part 1

Using details from the web below, draw a picture of an underwater setting.

a treasure chest   the ocean floor

many colorful fish   (Underwater)   light blue-green water

sea grasses   starfish

Write about five sentences describing the picture of the ocean that you just drew. Don't forget to include the details from the web.

Pick one of the following settings (or make up your own) and draw a picture of it in the box below.

haunted house

jungle

bedroom

My setting is _____.

Using the picture you just drew of a setting, write at least four details on the web below to describe your setting.

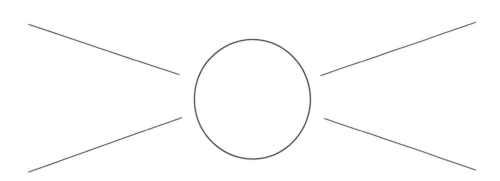

Now write about six sentences about your setting, using the details from the web above.

_____
_____
_____
_____
_____
_____
_____
_____
_____
_____
_____
_____
_____
_____
_____
_____
_____
_____

Content Review: Setting

1. Where does your story take place? _____

2. During what time of day does your story take place?

_____

_____

3. In what time of the year does your story take place?

_____

_____

Problem

Characters in a good story often face a **problem** (or conflict). A problem makes the story more interesting. This is because the reader wants to see what the characters will do to try to solve the problem.

•Practice

A good story often has a problem. Read this story and see if you can tell what the problem is:

Sam's Bunny

One October evening, Sam and his dad went to The Outdoor Market to pick out a pumpkin for Halloween. Sam brought his favorite stuffed animal with him. It was a bunny, and his name was Bunny. Later, when they got home, Sam realized he had left his bunny at The Outdoor Market. Sam was very upset because he could not go to sleep without Bunny.

They went back to The Outdoor Market, but it was closed. Sam and his dad peeked through the fence that surrounded The Outdoor Market. They could see the bunny sitting on top of a pumpkin. Sam started to cry. Dad told him not to worry, he had an idea.

They went home to get Dad's fishing rod. Dad was sure he could get the bunny.

Back at The Outdoor Market, Dad had to try many times, but finally he was able to hook the bunny on the end of his fishing line and reel it in over the top of the fence. Sam hugged Bunny tightly and they drove home.

What problem did Sam have?

_____

_____

_____

Read the story below. Then write the problem on the line after the story.

Sasha and Kate are cousins and play with each other a lot. One day when Kate was at Sasha's house, they decided it would be fun to watch a movie. Sasha picked one of her favorites and popped it into the VCR. Kate thought the movie was scary. She hated scary movies. Kate didn't want to spoil everyone's fun, so she didn't say anything. When she got home she told her mom.

What is the problem?

_____

_____

_____

_____

Who are the people in this story? (Who are the characters?)

_____

_____

_____

_____

Exercise 2

Read the story below and try to find the problem:

Alex lay in bed wondering what to wear to school. Today was her second day in the third grade. Her mom put out a pink and blue dress with flowers all over it, but Alex wanted to wear jeans and the new green sweater that her Uncle Tom gave her for her birthday. She thought for a moment, and then she realized that a sweater might be too hot. Alex's mother called her to come down and eat her breakfast, so she had to make a decision quickly. She finally put on her old jeans and a tee shirt, because she remembered that she had a plan to go worm hunting during recess with her friend Dan.

What problem did Alex have?

_____

_____

_____

_____

_____

Where does this story take place? (What is the setting?)

_____

_____

_____

_____

Create a problem for each of the main characters in the situations below. The first one is done for you.

Main Character   **Problem**

1. A girl who is going to a fair.   1. _____
                                          She has to find a
                                          _____
                                          babysitter for her sister.

2. A boy who went on a camping trip.   2. _____
                                          _____
                                          _____
                                          _____

3. A baby whale that goes swimming   3. _____
   with its mother.   _____
                                          _____
                                          _____

4. Ben, who has a soccer game on   4. _____
   Friday.   _____
                                          _____
                                          _____

Now choose one of the characters and problems from page 74. Write a short story about this character and the problem.

_____

- -

_____

- -

_____

- -

_____

- -

_____

- -

_____

- -

_____

- -

_____

- -

_____

- -

_____

- -

_____

- -

_____

- -

_____

- -

_____

- -

_____

- -

_____

Conclusion

A story needs an ending. The reader wants to know what happens to the characters. The ending is also called the **conclusion.** If there is a problem in the story, the conclusion tells whether it is solved.

• Practice

What does conclusion mean? A conclusion answers these questions:

1. How does the story end?
2. If there is a problem, does it get solved or not?
3. What happens to the main character or characters?
4. How does the character feel now?

Imagine how you would feel if you were watching an exciting TV show and someone unplugged the TV before the show was over. You'd probably be pretty upset! Most people want to know how a show ends. They want to know what happens to the characters. The same is true for stories you write. That's why stories need to be finished.

Now go back to page 71 and read the story about Sam's bunny again. What was the conclusion?

_____

_____

_____

_____

Read this short story and then write a conclusion. You may use one of the ideas at the bottom of the page to get started, and then add more sentences that tell about the conclusion. If you want, create your own idea and use that to write the ending.

Pam wanted to cheer up her grandmother. When Pam's grandfather passed away six months ago, her grandmother came to live with Pam and her family. Pam remembered when her grandmother was happier. She loved to play cards and do card tricks with Pam and her brother. They had so much fun! Pam wished she could get her grandmother to laugh and have fun again. With her brother, Pam looked around for their old pack of cards, but they couldn't find it.

_____

_____

_____

_____

_____

_____

_____

_____

_____

_____

_____

Ideas

1. Pam decided to ask her grandmother to watch a funny movie with her.

2. Pam decided to do some jobs around the house to earn the money to buy new cards. Then she would ask her grandmother to play with her.

Add an ending (conclusion) to these little stories.

1. Teresa is helping her Aunt Rosa clean out the attic. Aunt Rosa wants to get rid of an old trunk, but it is very heavy. How can they get it downstairs? _____

_____

_____

_____

_____

2. For his school project, Ray tried to build a castle out of gumdrops. Pieces of candy kept disappearing from the castle as he built it! What happened and what did Ray do about it? _____

_____

_____

_____

_____

Exercise 3

A conclusion can solve a problem and bring an end to the story. Write a conclusion to this story:

Yesterday, Marisa woke up late. Her alarm clock had broken! She was very upset, because she didn't want to be late for school. Quickly, she jumped out of bed, got dressed, and had some orange juice. Carrying a bagel in one hand and her school bag in the other, Marisa ran down Chestnut Street to the bus stop. After waiting for five minutes, she realized she had missed her bus. _____

_____

_____

_____

_____

_____

_____

_____

Story Plan

✎ Here is a blank story plan for you to use for your next story.

If you are not sure what to write about, you can use the list of story starters on page 140 to help you get started. If you know what you want to write about, make a story plan with an idea of your own.

Topic: _____

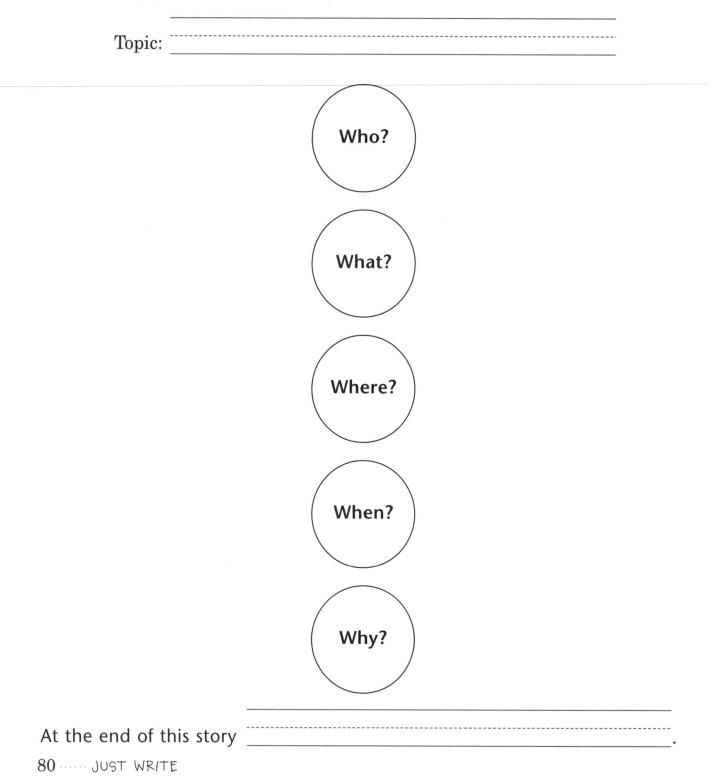

At the end of this story _____.

Now write your own short story, using the plan you made on page 80.

Content Review: Problem and Conclusion

Think about your story by answering these questions:

1. What is the problem?

_____

_____

2. Does the problem get solved?

_____

_____

3. If it does, how does the problem get solved?

_____

_____

_____

4. If it doesn't, what is your conclusion?

_____

_____

_____

Chapter 3
Capitals and Basic Punctuation

Now that you've had some practice writing sentences and stories, you can focus on other parts of writing. After you've brainstormed and written down some ideas, you want to think about how to make your story clear to the reader. It's important to use capital letters and punctuation to help your readers know where one sentence ends and a new one begins. This will make it easier for people to read your story.

It doesn't matter if you use capitals and punctuation when you're just writing down ideas. Your ideas are just for you. But if you want your story to make sense and be easy to read, you should use capitals and punctuation.

Capitals

Always use a capital letter at the beginning of a sentence. This helps your readers see where a new sentence begins.

Also use a capital letter for the names of your characters: Alison, Papa Bear, Jose, Bert, Floyd, Tuck.

I like to write Punctuation

- Use a period at the end of a sentence that makes a statement.
- Use a question mark at the end of a sentence that asks a question.
- Use an exclamation mark at the end of a sentence to express a strong feeling.

These different types of punctuation also help your reader by making it easier to understand the feeling in the sentence.

Here are three examples of sentences. Each one begins with a capital letter and each one ends with punctuation—a period, a question mark, or an exclamation mark.

Statement: In the summer, Rosanna likes to play basketball.

Question: Do you want to play in the mud?

Strong feeling: I am so excited about this movie!

•Practice

Remember, when you write a sentence:

> Begin it with a capital letter.

> End it with punctuation.

✎Rewrite these sentences with a capital letter at the beginning and the correct punctuation at the end.

1. my new sneakers are red

_____

- -

_____

2. that movie was so funny

_____

- -

_____

3. did you bring me a surprise

_____

- -

_____

Remember, sentences usually end with a period, question mark, or exclamation mark.

> Let's go for a bike ride this weekend.

> Do you need air in your bike tires?

> Look out for that pothole!

At the beginning of each sentence, cross out the lowercase letter and write a capital letter. Then put the correct punctuation mark at the end. The first one is done for you.

1. Are there any cookies left?

2. hurry or we will miss the school bus

3. what will we do

4. they danced and played all day

5. can I play, too

6. patrick climbed down the rocky path

7. wow, that was so much fun

8. where are we

Chapter 4
Using Your Senses

When we write, we should use words that have to do with our five senses. The senses are

> seeing
>
> smelling
>
> hearing
>
> touching
>
> tasting

Using "sense words" will make your story seem real. In their minds, your readers will be able to see the things you describe, hear the sounds you write about, or maybe smell the meal you're describing.

• Practice

When you write, you should use words that have to do with the senses. Remember, the senses are

seeing

smelling

hearing

touching

tasting

Read this list and circle the phrases that have to do with seeing:

a big smile

a funny movie

happy thoughts

a great idea

a clear, blue sky

a red jumper

Read this list and circle the phrases that have to do with smelling:

a stinky fish

a large book

a smoky fire

a red car

a pigpen

freshly baked cookies

Read this list and circle the phrases that have to do with hearing:

a squealing brake

a tall tree

pounding hammers

a sweet orange

loud voices

jingling bells

Read this list and circle the phrases that have to do with touching:

a smooth rock

a big TV

a prickly pinecone

a funny story

soft rabbit fur

a long movie

Read this list and circle the phrases that have to do with tasting:

a sour lemon

sweet honey

a wooden table

a small box

frosty ice cubes

salt water

Read the story below.

Erin's Day at the Circus

My mom and I went in the dark circus tent. Soon colored lights sparkled everywhere and the announcer's voice boomed out. I could smell the delicious, buttery popcorn we had bought. I had to have a bite of the warm, salty snack. Then an elephant entered the circus ring and let out a loud roar. On his back he carried a clown in a purple suit. The elephant slowly walked over to my mom. He stopped and looked at her for a minute, and then his long trunk came forward and suddenly snatched our popcorn! She gasped and stared down in disbelief at her empty hands. We were both very surprised! I grabbed my mom's arm, and we both looked at each other and started to laugh. I loved our day at the circus.

1. What could Erin hear?

2. What did she touch?

3. Write three things that Erin could see.

4. What could Erin smell?

5. What did Erin taste?

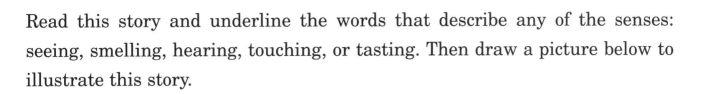

Exercise 2

Read this story and underline the words that describe any of the senses: seeing, smelling, hearing, touching, or tasting. Then draw a picture below to illustrate this story.

A Surprising Sail

Saturday morning, we decided to go for a sail. When we started out, there was a gentle breeze, the sun was warm, and the sky was bright blue. Seagulls called to each other and coasted on the wind.

Suddenly, clouds moved in and the sky got very dark. The wind picked up and the waves splashed salty, cold water in our faces. My dad yelled, "Look out!" and brought the sail crashing down. When he started the engine, we heard its gentle hum. Soon, we were safely in the harbor.

Get ready to use all five senses in your next story. Write the topic and details below.

The topic is _____.

Who or what will you see?

_____

Write two of the details you will use to describe what you saw.

_____

Write one thing you will smell in your story.

_____

Write one thing you will taste.

_____

Write two things you will touch in your story.

_____

Write two things you will hear.

_____

Now use what you wrote in part 1 to write a story that describes what you see, smell, hear, touch, and taste.

_____

_____

_____

_____

_____

_____

_____

_____

_____

_____

_____

_____

_____

_____

_____

_____

_____

_____

_____

_____

Practice writing about using your senses as you fill in the blanks in the sentences below.

When I opened the door, I could see it was still raining and the wind was blowing hard. The air smelled _____. I could hear the sound of _____. When I walked out to the barn, my sneakers got soaking wet. My feet felt _____. After I tried to open the gate, my hands felt _____. Once I got inside the barn, I saw _____ and _____. I could also smell _____.

Last Saturday was a beautiful day. Hanna and I went to the playground. As soon as we got there, I saw _____. There were other kids playing on the playground. I could hear them _____. Hanna and I ran down to the pond. The wet grass felt _____, and it made a squeaky noise when we ran. We watched the ducks swimming, but then I slipped and fell into the duck pond! The water was _____ and _____.

Chapter 5
Paragraphs

A **paragraph** is usually three or four sentences that tell about the topic. Each sentence gives you some information about the topic.

✎ Practice

Reread the story "A Surprising Sail" on page 91. Do you see how it is broken into two parts? Why do you think it is broken like this?

_____

_____

A new paragraph shows a slight change in the writer's mind. Breaking your story into paragraphs helps your reader to know that something in your story has changed. In "A Surprising Sail," some time goes by between paragraph 1 and paragraph 2. The weather also changes. The new paragraph helps make these changes clear.

Here is a passage that should be written in two paragraphs. Notice where a change happens. A | between sentences shows where a new paragraph should begin.

There are many types of apples. Some are sweet and tasty. Others are so tart and small that they are not good for people to eat, but they are wonderful for the birds. | There are also many kinds of oranges. Some are great for making juice. Navel oranges are perfect for peeling and eating. Tangelos are a mixture of an orange and a tangerine. They are also juicy and delicious.

This is how it should look:

There are many types of apples. Some are sweet and tasty. Others are so tart and small that they are not good for people to eat, but they are wonderful for the birds.

There are also many kinds of oranges. Some are great for making juice. Navel oranges are perfect for peeling and eating. Tangelos are a mixture of an orange and a tangerine. They are also juicy and delicious.

Read the story below. Find the place where the change happens, and draw a line between sentences to show where the story should be broken into two paragraphs.

When Mark was in the second grade, he lived in Tennessee. His neighbor, Erik, was his good friend. Together with Erik's older brother, the boys built a tree house. They called it their clubhouse. They liked to bring snacks up there and trade baseball cards. Ten years later, Mark came back to Tennessee to go to Erik's high school graduation. The two friends thought it would be fun to visit their old tree house. They climbed up the ladder, which was still strong, but when they got to the clubhouse, they saw that birds' nests occupied the little room. Each corner was heavy with cobwebs from the spiders that had moved in. Erik noticed a few old cards still on the table. Mark and Erik smiled as they remembered back to when they were in the second grade.

Indenting

Indenting is a way to show the beginning of a new paragraph. When you indent, you begin the first sentence of a paragraph with about two fingers' width of space from the left side of your paper. Look at the drawing below:

The extra space makes it easy to see where a new paragraph starts.

• Practice

Read the paragraph below. The first sentence of the paragraph is indented. Notice that each sentence begins with a capital letter and ends with a different punctuation mark.

The Red Sox play the Yankees tonight. I can't wait! If our team beats them, we will win the series. Do you know what time the game begins?

Now rewrite the three-sentence paragraph below. Remember what you have learned about indenting, capitals, and punctuation.

did your ball just roll into the street wait, there's a car coming you can get it when the light changes

_____

_____

_____

_____

Topic Sentence

A **topic sentence** tells the reader what the paragraph is about. It describes the main idea of the paragraph.

Read the paragraph below. The topic sentence has been underlined for you. The topic of the paragraph is ears. The main idea is the shapes and sizes of animals' ears.

<u>Ears come in many shapes and sizes.</u> The African elephant's ear can measure as much as three feet across. A little North African fox has wide ears that are about three inches tall. A rabbit's narrow ears are about four inches long.

•Practice

Read the paragraph below and underline the topic sentence.

It's important to put your garden in a good place in the yard. It should be in a spot that has at least six hours of sun a day. It should be far enough away from trees so that the trees' roots don't take away the soil's water and food that help plants grow. If the garden is on too steep a hill, the soil and the food in it can wash away in the rain.

Exercise 1

Read these paragraphs below and underline the topic sentence for each one.

1.   The White House is a famous American building. It contains the home and office of the president of the United States. It is located in Washington, D.C., at 1600 Pennsylvania Avenue. The Lincoln Bedroom is one of its famous rooms. Every year, many people tour the White House.

2.   Max is my best friend. We usually ride our bikes down to the park on Saturdays. He never forgets my birthday. We both love funny movies. My dad says I am lucky to have a good friend like Max.

Exercise 2

Remember, a topic sentence tells the main idea of the paragraph.

In the exercises below, you will see that each paragraph needs a topic sentence. Only the details have been given. At the end of each selection, choose the best topic sentence and write it on the line at the top. The first one has been done for you.

1. **There is a lot of equipment on our playground.**

   The swing set has a big slide. Some like to play in the sandbox, but I love the tree house. There are two basketball nets and a lot of balls.

   a. It's fun to practice basketball.

   b. There is a lot of equipment on our playground.

   c. The tree house has two doors.

2. _____

   We have a book of maps and many books about faraway places. My sister has lots of books of make-believe stories. Some books are about real people.

   a. My dad likes to read about history.

   b. I like reading adventure stories.

   c. There are many kinds of books.

3. _____

   Mario comes from Mexico. Kala moved here from Haiti. Pedro lived in Peru until last year.

   a. I might visit Mario this summer.

   b. My friends come from many different places.

   c. Peru is in South America.

At the end of each selection, choose the best topic sentence and write it on the line at the top.

1. _____

You can play a board game with your brother or sister. You can put on a puppet show for your mom and dad. You can read a good book.

    a. Many people love to read.

    b. There is a lot you can do on a rainy day.

    c. Brothers are fun to play with.

2. _____

My mom has a yummy grilled chicken recipe. My dad cooks bluefish on the grill. My sister and I love hamburgers and hot dogs cooked on the grill.

    a. We love to use our grill.

    b. There are several different kinds of outdoor grills.

    c. I hope we have chicken for dinner tonight.

3. _____

The wolf is a carnivore, which means it eats only meat. The lion has strong jaws and teeth because it is a meat eater. The tiger is another well-known meat eater.

    a. Giraffes do not eat meat.

    b. Some animals only eat meat.

    c. My friend saw a family of wolves in Canada.

Supporting Details

Supporting details tell more about the topic sentence. They give support, or reasons, for why the topic sentence is true.

• Practice

Read the following paragraph:

> The blue whale is a huge animal. It is the largest animal on earth. It is usually about 100 feet long. A blue whale can weigh as much as 150 tons!

The three sentences after the topic sentence give more information about the topic sentence, and they help the reader understand why the blue whale is such a large animal.

In the exercise below, the supporting details are given. Write a topic sentence on the line above each group. The first one is done for you.

1. **_It is very cold in Antarctica._**

   The lowest temperature recorded in Antarctica was –126.9 degrees.

   People must wear special clothes to keep warm there.

   In Antarctica, people must eat large quantities of food to fuel their bodies.

   A cold wind whirls off the immense polar ice dome.

2. _____

   Most snakes are harmless to people.

   Some snakes are poisonous.

   A python can squeeze its prey to death.

   The anaconda can eat an animal whole.

3. _____

   Mom drives us to the mountains.

   I always wear hiking boots for climbing.

   The hiking trails are clearly marked.

   Climbing to the top makes us hungry.

In the exercises below, the supporting details are given. Write a topic sentence on the line above each group. The first one is done for you.

1. <u>*The porcupine is a strange animal.*</u>

Porcupines' legs turn in, so they often step on their own toes.

A porcupine can't run; it only waddles.

Porcupines are covered with sharp, pointed quills.

The porcupine's small black eyes can only see things that are close.

2. _____

Cockroaches are bugs that carry germs.

Cockroaches don't eat much, but they spoil food.

Cockroaches hide, but they live around humans for their warmth and food.

People often squash cockroaches.

3. _____

We need water when we are thirsty.

People use water for cooking and cleaning the dishes.

We also use water for showering or bathing.

We have to have water to brush our teeth.

After reading the supporting details, write a good topic sentence on the line above each group.

1. _____

Grandma can cook really good spaghetti sauce.

She loves to do puzzles and play cards.

Grandma likes taking my sister and me to the movies.

2. _____

There are toys and clothes all over my cousin's room.

Her bed is unmade.

Her desk is covered with messy papers, crayons, and glue.

3. _____

I am supposed to take the trash out every Wednesday.

I walk the dog each day after school.

In the summer, my big job is to water the vegetable garden every morning.

A good paragraph needs details to support the topic sentence. Without the details, it is difficult for the reader to believe the topic sentence.

Underline the topic sentence in the following paragraph.

> The giraffe is the tallest animal. He is so tall that he can reach food that most other animals can't reach. Being tall also helps him to see if danger is close by. He can see way over and beyond other animals. The giraffe's long neck and long legs are very useful to him.

Write two of the supporting details about the topic sentence from the story above.

1. _____

2. _____

Write three details about each topic sentence. For the third topic sentence, fill in the blank with your favorite activity (such as playing soccer), and then give three supporting details about why you like it.

1. Cold food is great to eat when it is hot out.

a. _____

b. _____

c. _____

2. People celebrate many different holidays.

a. _____

b. _____

c. _____

3. My favorite activity is _____ .

a. _____

b. _____

c. _____

✎ Exercise 6

Write three details about each topic sentence. For the last sentence, fill in the blank with your favorite time of the year and then give supporting details about why it's your favorite.

1. There are lots of things to do at recess.

a. _____

b. _____

c. _____

2. There are many different languages in the world.

   a. _____

   b. _____

   c. _____

3. My favorite time of the year is _____.

   a. _____

   b. _____

   c. _____

✎ Exercise 7, part 1

Pick a topic from the list below. Write your topic sentence on the lines on page 110 and then add three supporting details about the topic.

a food I like

chores at home

having a cold

making paper airplanes

weekend activities

sports heroes

my favorite shirt

Topic Sentence: _____

1. _____

2. _____

3. _____

Now, think of your own topic and write it on the line below. Then write a topic sentence and three supporting details about it.

Topic: _____

Topic Sentence: _____

1. _____

2. _____

3. _____

Choose one of your topics from page 110. Using your topic sentence and your supporting details, write a paragraph. Don't forget to use capitals and punctuation!

Chapter 6
Telling More

Giving more information (details) can make your writing more interesting. Thinking about the words *who, what, where, when, why,* and *how* can help you tell your readers more about what is happening in the story. When you give interesting details, people will really enjoy reading your stories.

Expanding with Details

Remember this basic sentence?

   The dog barked.

We used words such as *who, what, where, when, why,* and *how* to tell the reader more about what was happening:

   The dog on the porch barked fiercely last night because he heard a noise.

In this chapter you will practice adding details like these to make your sentences more engaging.

✎ Practice

Think of details for the sentences below, using *who, what, where, when, why,* and *how*. Then rewrite the sentence and include your detail.

1. Add details to this sentence to tell *who*.

    She loves math problems.

Detail:

_____

_____

Rewritten sentence:

_____

_____

_____

_____

2. Add details to this sentence to tell *what*.

    Alan likes to read.

Detail:

_____

_____

Rewritten sentence:

_____

_____

_____

_____

3. Add details to this sentence to tell *where*.

We played soccer.

Detail:

_____

_____

Rewritten sentence:

_____

_____

_____

_____

4. Add details to this sentence to tell *when*.

My grandmother visited.

Detail:

_____

_____

Rewritten sentence:

_____

_____

_____

_____

5. Add details to this sentence to tell *why*.

The electricity went out.

Detail:

_____

_____

Rewritten sentence:

_____

_____

_____

_____

6. Add details to this sentence to tell *how*.

I opened the box.

Detail:

_____

_____

Rewritten sentence:

_____

_____

_____

_____

Read this boring paragraph:

My best birthday present this year was from my brother. He got me tickets to a game. It was fun. We had some great food.

Using *who, what, where, when, why,* and *how,* we added details to the paragraph. Now read the improved paragraph below and notice how much more interesting it is with the details.

My best birthday present this year was from my older brother, Lee. He gave me tickets to see the Lakers play basketball. Part of the present was that he would take me to the game. Lee is really fun to be with, but I don't get to do that much with him because he is much older than I am. I was really excited because I had never been to a night game before. We drove to the Staples Center in Los Angeles. Lee got us great seats right behind the team bench. We each had popcorn and hot dogs. We were so happy when the Lakers won.

Read this boring paragraph:

> My bedroom is nice. I share it with my sister. I have a nice bedspread. My curtains are white.

Now read the improved paragraph below and notice how much more interesting it is with the added details.

> My sister and I share a great bedroom. It is cozy and pretty. The walls and ceiling are sky blue, and our mom painted clouds on the ceiling. Fluffy white curtains frame the window. The room is small, but we fit in two beds, a desk, and a bureau. Our grandmother made us beautiful quilts to use as bedspreads. I like to keep my toys and stuffed animals set up in my own way. You have to be invited to come into our room.

1. Why does she think her bedroom is great?

_____

_____

2. What did their mom paint on the ceiling?

_____

_____

3. Who made her quilt?

_____

_____

Read this boring paragraph.

> We played in a tournament. I scored the winning goal. My team won a trophy.

Now expand this paragraph with details. Here are some questions to help you.

What sport is it? _____

What is the name of your team? _____

Where did you play? _____

How did you feel when you won?

_____

_____

_____

Now rewrite the paragraph above and add these details to make it more interesting. Don't forget to indent the first sentence.

_____

_____

_____

_____

_____

_____

_____

_____

_____

Exercise 4

Read the following paragraphs. You will notice that each paragraph is missing details. In the spaces provided, add more information to make a better paragraph.

1.   Last Saturday I stayed at my cousin's house. My cousin and I had _____

so much fun. _____

_____

_____

_____

_____

_____

I hope that I will be able to go to my cousin's again soon.

2.   Marc loves to draw. _____

_____

His Aunt Mary Anne gave him a set of colored pencils. Marc saved

allowance and bought a pad of good drawing paper. _____

_____

He gave his Aunt Mary Anne a beautiful picture to thank her for her

gift.

Here are two more paragraphs that need details. In the space provided, add information to make a better paragraph.

1.   Today, Travis was very foolish. He left his apartment in a rush. He forgot to turn off the oven, and he left the milk and cold cuts out on the counter, where the dog could reach them. _____
_____
_____
_____

When Travis got home in the afternoon, the apartment was a mess.
_____
_____
_____
_____
_____
_____

2.   Yesterday was a really hot, summery day. _____
_____
_____
_____

The sun shone like a ball of fire. _____
_____
_____

I decided to go to the library, where the air conditioning kept me cool and comfortable.

Dario is going to write a paragraph about his uncle. Here are some of the details that he wants to include.

> great cook
>
> loves to tell stories to my sister and me
>
> will play games with me
>
> likes to play the piano

Think about a sentence that describes the main idea of Dario's paragraph. Then write a good topic sentence on the line below.

_____
- -
_____

Now write the whole paragraph with sentences using the details above. Rewrite the topic sentence at the beginning of the paragraph first, and then write the rest of the sentences. Remember to indent when you begin writing.

_____
- -
_____

_____
- -
_____

_____
- -
_____

_____
- -
_____

_____
- -
_____

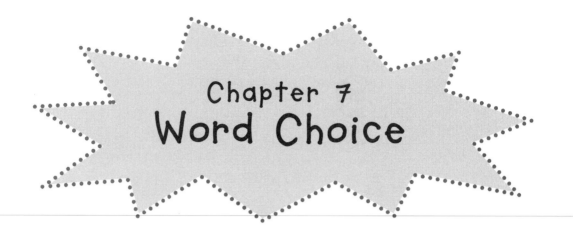

Chapter 7
Word Choice

Your writing needs interesting words. If you use the same common words over and over, the writing becomes dull, and your reader will get bored. There are lots of ways to have fun with words. In this chapter, you will practice describing things and people with different words.

• Practice

While you read this paragraph, notice the choice of words.

> From my bedroom upstairs, I heard the splattering, crashing sound of glass breaking. My ears strained to hear more. Then I heard footsteps darting back and forth and my dad's sturdy voice lecturing Tilly, our cat. He spoke very firmly. My guess was that Tilly had accidentally broken something again. Although she could gracefully spring up to counters and tabletops, her long, bushy tail had a way of sweeping anything in her way to the floor. We all love Tilly, but sometimes she is truly annoying.

Now underline some of the most interesting, different words.

Overused Words

Sometimes people write the same words over and over in their stories. Some words that are used too much are *said, good, nice,* and *bad.* These words become boring if you use them all the time. Try to use different words that are more interesting than these words. (That doesn't mean you can *never* use these words—just use other words as well.)

Said

Some writers use the word *said* too often. The following words are good replacements for *said.*

Suggestions to replace *said:*

declared	explained
answered	remarked
whispered	shouted
asked	replied
screamed	chuckled
hollered	commented
yelled	grumbled

In the dialogue below, cross out the word *said* and write a replacement above it. You can use words from the list on page 123 or words that you think of on your own.

"I am so excited that we won our soccer game!" said Julio.

"You played really well," said the coach.

While running home, Julio said to his friends, "Hey, we won!"

"Wow, that is great!" said Elena.

"Did you score?" said Fred.

"No," said Julio.

"I heard your shoe fell off when you kicked the ball," said Elena.

"Yes, my shoe was untied," said Julio.

"That's the funniest thing I ever heard," said Fred.

"Don't laugh at me," said Julio.

"Sorry, I didn't mean to laugh. You are a good soccer player," said Fred.

Bad

Bad is another common word that is often used too much. Here are some good substitutes for it:

terrible   nervous

awful   sad

horrible   boring

difficult   nasty

✎ Exercise 2

Read this paragraph and then cross out each *bad* and replace it with another word. If you need help, look at the words above.

Today was a bad day. First of all, I felt bad as soon as I woke. My

throat hurt and my head felt bad. My mom made me stay in bed all

day and that was bad! A friend called in the afternoon and said that

they had a bad math test in school. That made me feel bad, because

I know I will have to take the test when I go back to school.

Good and Nice

Good and *nice* are two other common words that are used too often. Using these substitutes will make your writing more interesting.

friendly	wonderful
cute	exciting
silly	incredible
thoughtful	excellent
adorable	fantastic
amazing	

Exercise 3

Read this paragraph and fill in the blanks. Do not use *good* or *nice*. Look at the list above if you need to.

The O'Hara family is really _____. My friend Megan O'Hara is a _____ girl. Her dad and mine are friends, too. It was so _____ when she and her dad came to visit yesterday. Abby, her baby sister, came with them. It can be so _____ when we play with our baby sisters. The babies are really _____. Together Megan and I read them stories and set up their toys while our dads cooked a _____ lunch. We all had a _____ time. It was _____ the way the babies giggled and played together.

Using Comparisons

When you choose words to describe something, you can make your writing more powerful when you compare one person or thing to something else. Read these examples:

She is as light as a feather. (She is being compared to a feather.)

John is as fast as a racecar. (John is being compared to a racecar.)

This penny shines like gold. (The penny is being compared to _____.)

When you want to use a comparison, you must think of something that both things have in common. For example, John and a racecar are both very fast. Be creative!

✎ Practice

Complete the following sentences using creative comparisons.

1. My hands are as cold as _____.

2. He felt as small as a _____.

3. The alarm ringing sounded like _____.

4. The library was as quiet as _____.

5. The rug was furry like a _____.

✎ Exercise 1

Use creative comparisons to finish these sentences.

1. The blanket was as soft as a _____.

2. The witch was as mean as a _____.

3. She ran like a _____.

4. He was as tall as a _____.

5. The rock was round like a _____.

6. The ball went as fast as a _____.

✎ Exercise 2

Now write your own paragraph. Use interesting word choices (no overused words) and at least three creative comparisons. If you get stuck, look back at the examples. Don't forget to indent and to use capital letters and punctuation.

_____

_____

_____

_____

_____

_____

_____

_____

Writing an ad is a fun way to practice using interesting words. An advertisement tries to persuade you to buy something. It uses different words and appeals to your senses to try to catch your attention.

Read this ad:

> Sparkle toothpaste makes your mouth taste fresh. Your bright smile will sparkle because your teeth will be whiter and cleaner than ever.

Underline the words that try to catch your attention and persuade you to use Sparkle.

Read the next ad:

> Do your feet feel tired and worn out at the end of a long day? Sit back and slip your feet into some Comfy Slippers. You will feel instantly refreshed and rested. You will love them so much that you will want to rush out and buy a pair of Comfies for a friend.

Underline the words that try to get you to wear Comfy Slippers.

Write Your Own Ad

Now write your own advertisement that will make or persuade someone to buy your product. Choose an idea from the list below or write an ad for something that you think up. Write the name of your product on the blank line, and then write the ad. When you are done, draw a picture of your product.

markers   a new kind of cereal

a new toy   an ice cream topping

_____

A book review tells people about a book you have read. If you liked the book and you write a good review, other people will want to read that book. Write a review for a favorite book that would make a friend want to read it. If you want, draw a picture on a separate piece of paper to go with your review.

Chapter 8
Editing and Publishing

After you have written a story, it's a good idea to read it again to see if there's any way you can make it even better. When it is as good as you can make it, you can turn the story into a book by adding a cover and pictures, if you want.

Selecting a Story

The first step is to choose one of the stories you have written in this book. This is the one you will publish. Find the story that you think is the most interesting, or the one that was the most fun to write.

Revising the Content

The second step is to make sure the content makes sense. You've already practiced this with the Content Revision checklists. Just make sure you haven't left anything out. Don't worry yet about punctuation, spelling, or capital letters.

Check your writing by reading your story out loud. Listen to yourself as you read and make sure what you have written is clear. Your ears often pick up what your eyes don't see.

•Practice

Content Checklist

Read the story you have chosen again. Then look at the items in this checklist. Can you think of anything that you want to add to your story?

_____ 1. Does your story have a clear topic?

_____ 2. Does the sequence of the story make sense?

_____ 3. Have you included at least two or three interesting details about your character?

_____ 4. Did you show your character's feelings about what is happening?

_____ 5. Did you tell where or when the story took place?

_____ 6. Does your character have a problem?

_____ 7. Did you include any senses?

_____ 8. Did you make good word choices?

_____ 9. Did you use any comparisons?

_____ 10. Do you have an interesting conclusion to your story?

Using the same story as in the checklist on page 133, answer the following questions.

1. Where does your story take place? _____

_____

2. In what time of the year or time of day does your story take place?

_____

_____

3. Give two or three interesting details about your characters.

_____

_____

_____

_____

_____

4. What feelings do your characters show?

_____

_____

5. What is the main idea of your story?

_____

_____

6. What are some details you have used to support the main idea?

_____

_____

7. What senses did you use in your story?

_____

_____

8. Is the conclusion happy, sad, or another emotion?

_____

_____

Editing

The next step is to check your punctuation and capital letters to make sure you have used them correctly. Check the spelling of any words that you think you might have spelled wrong. Use classroom resources such as dictionaries and textbooks, or ask your teacher for help. It's a good idea to keep a list of words you use often in your writing. Then you can just look at your list when you're not sure how to spell a word.

Editing Checklist

_____1. Sentences and characters' names begin with capital letters.

_____2. Sentences have correct punctuation.

_____3. Paragraphs are indented.

_____4. Misspelled words are corrected or underlined.

On the page that has your story, write the changes you need to make. Try to write neatly so that you can still read your story easily after you make the changes. Be sure you've added all the new words you want to include. Fix your spelling, punctuation, and capitalization if you need to. Then read your story out loud again. Make sure your new changes make sense.

•Practice

Now swap stories with a classmate. Use the checklist above to help each other see if you've missed anything.

Choosing a Title

If you haven't already given your story a title, now is the time. Some writers like to wait until they are finished writing the story, and then they think of a title. Others like to think of the title first and then write the story. Either way is fine.

If you are having trouble thinking of a title, ask yourself some questions:

Who is the main character in my story?

What happens to this character?

Is there an event that is the most important thing in the story? (For example, the important event in "Erin's Day at the Circus," page 90, is the trip to the circus.)

Try to think of creative titles for your stories. For example, "A Surprising Sail" is a more interesting title than "The Day I Went Sailing" or "My Sailing Trip." If you are stuck, don't be afraid to give your story a simple title (such as "Lions"). Then change it later if you think of a better one (such as "The Lion's Roar").

Publishing

It's fun to publish a story by making it into a real book. You can add illustrations, include an "About the Author" page, and make a colorful cover.

You need to follow several steps to publish your story:

1. Choose one of your favorite stories that you have written.

2. Complete the Content Checklist.

3. Complete the Editing Checklist.

4. Write the changes you need to make on your story page.

5. Write a final draft of your story. This means that you will rewrite your story on a separate piece of paper and include all the changes and corrections you have made. Use your best handwriting, so your story is easy to read.

6. Write some facts about yourself on the "About the Author" form (page 138) and use that form to write a paragraph. Include that paragraph with your story. If you want, draw a picture of yourself or paste a photo on that page.

7. Make your cover. You can use crayons, markers, glitter, colored paper, or any other supplies in your classroom.

8. Staple your book together, or tie the pages and cover together with yarn or string.

Now your book is ready to share with your classmates, friends, or family. Congratulations!

About the Author

✎Fill out the form below. Then use it to plan an "About the Author" paragraph that you will include in your published book. (You can include other information about yourself, too.) Write your paragraph on a separate piece of paper and place it at the end of your book.

Name _____

Your age _____

Where you live _____

Where you go to school _____

What you like to do in your free time _____

_____

Your favorite things to write about _____

_____

_____

My Brainstorming Ideas

Story Starters

1. My sister said that she saw bright yellow eyes peeking at her from under her bed.

2. One day I took a trip in a hot air balloon . . .

3. I wasn't sure if I should go in the lake.

4. Something unexpected happened at my birthday party.

5. When I opened the kitchen door, there was a strange smell in the air.

6. Alan couldn't believe his eyes when . . .

7. One day, three kids discovered an old trunk in their garage.

Here is space to write some of your own story starters.

_____

_____

_____

_____

_____

_____

_____

_____